Spiritual Father

or

Spiritual Failure

by
Dr. Michael P. Jacobs

Spiritual Father or Spiritual Failure
ISBN   978-0-97198-351-9
Copyright © 2005 by Dr. Michael P. Jacobs
Church on the Rock
4224 Mel Smith Road
New Albany, Indiana 47150

Recommendations

As a pastor, I know the heartbreak that can come into the lives of people when they make wrong associations; but on the other hand, the blessing of having right associations in your life is limitless! When God moves to bless your life, He sends a person; when the enemy moves to harm your life, he sends a person! Knowing which associations will make fruitful impartations is imperative to a successful life and ministry.

Pastor Michael Jacobs helps us to identify those God-sent people, and to successfully cooperate with the supply they can bring to our lives. Pastor Jacobs skillfully brings this revelation to the forefront in simplicity. In reading this book, you will learn in a short time what otherwise, could have taken you years to learn on your own; and will prove to be invaluable as you faithfully run your race.

Pastor Nancy Dufresne
World Harvest Church
Murrieta, California

This book is a timely revelation that we feel must be in the hands of every believer! These spiritual truths that have been penned in this book will change your life as it has ours. We cannot even begin to express in words the value of having a spiritual father and how that has revolutionized our life and ministry! We have experienced first hand the fruit that has come from us being properly connected to our spiritual father! As you begin to study these biblical truths you will begin to see the value and importance of having a spiritual father.

Thank-you, Pastor Michael for writing this book and for being our pastor! It is truly an honor to be called your spiritual children!

Dr. Dennis and Pastor Angela Hattabaugh
Church on the Rock
Georgetown, Texas

God is a wise investor who wants each of His children to achieve their maximum potential. *Spiritual Father or Spiritual Failure* reminds us that achieving success in the kingdom is never fully attributed to gifting, calling or special ability alone. Our fulfillment of purpose and the key to releasing God's greatest blessings into our lives, is being "hooked-up" to a spiritual supply. We call these supplies, "fathers in the faith." With insightful clarity, Pastor Jacobs establishes God's biblical pattern for spiritual fathers and sons and instructs us in the principles of honor. Both fathers and sons; ministers and lay persons will gain great understanding of the responsibility and great blessing that comes along with establishing and maintaining this precious covenant connection. It is a profound honor to be able to endorse this book. Both as a lovingly executed word of the Spirit and as a practical guidebook for the body of Christ's success.

Pastors Johnny and Debra Simons
Harvest Two Outreach
Merced, California

Thank you for being our spiritual father in the Lord. The spiritual deposits that you and Pastor Diana made in our lives for 20 years has helped us find our ministry in the Lord. It took nothing less for God to transform us spiritually and emotionally as you taught and demonstrated His Word. May this book help others to obtain the success in their service to the Lord as they find and follow their spiritual father.

Pastors Keith and Cynthia Rogan
Church on the Rock Nashville
Nashville, Tennessee

Table of Contents

Foreword

I appreciate Dr. Michael Jacobs writing on this all-important subject because few realize the importance of divine connections that God wants to bring into our lives. These divine connections with other spiritual leaders are to be an umbrella of blessing over our lives.

God's plan is that each of us run our race and finish in full success, but we can't do that alone - and that's why God gives us these divine connections. As Paul wrote to the church in Rome saying, *"For I long to see you, that I may IMPART unto you some spiritual gift, to the END ye may be established"*, he was letting them know that their "end" was dependent on the "impartations" they were to receive through him. Without those impartations, their outcome, their "end", would be different. Few Christians realize that their blessing is connected to another man. All through scripture, we see divine alliances that were authored by God; they were powerful in function, and far-reaching in blessing. There was Moses and Joshua, Elijah and Elisha, and Paul and Timothy; men who worked together, prayed together, and made a difference - together!

Psalm 127:4 reads, *"As arrows are in the hand of a mighty man; so are the children of the youth."* A mighty man of war is able to send an arrow in the direction that hits the target. This is what a good father does with his children - he helps them to hit God's target for their life. Likewise, a man who is mighty in spiritual things is able to guide those of his association in the direction that will enable them to hit their target!

Where do believers so often miss it? They don't stay close enough to those spiritual leaders who can help them secure their aim and direction.

My own life and ministry is a reflection of the divine connections that God brought into my own life. Kenneth Hagin and Dr. Lester Sumrall were divine connections who made impartations into me through their teachings, through conversations, and their examples in living. My life would look different without the divine supply they brought to my life.

Are you serious about fulfilling God's plan for your life? You can't do it alone!

Jesus is all you need for your redemption, but Jesus gave the fivefold offices to help you mature in Christ, and to mature in your office and divine assignments. It's your job to know who those divine supplies are that God brings into your life, and not forfeit their divine association as long as they follow Christ, for your outcome depends on it. What will you be? Someone with a *"Spiritual Father or a Spiritual Failure?"*

Dr. Jacobs not only writes to you from years of experience, but he writes to you from the position of himself being a faithful spiritual son. He's not just a man with a revelation, but a man who lives this revelation.

Dr. Ed Dufresne
Ed Dufresne Ministries
Murrieta, California

Introduction

*For though ye have ten thousand instructors
in Christ, yet have ye not many fathers: for
in Christ Jesus I have begotten you through
the gospel. (1 Corinthians 4:15)*

It was 1994 and I had been in full-time ministry for twenty years. I was the senior pastor of a strong local church and had traveled on over 40 mission trips. Still, something was missing. I knew that God was calling me to a new phase of ministry, but I did not know how to get there. Something that I vitally needed to make that step was missing. I needed clarity. While in prayer one day God said, *"Contact Dr. Ed Dufresne and have him come to your church."* This led to a divine appointment. I did not realize it at the time, but God had an impartation for me. He delivered that impartation through a man. My help had come. Over lunch during those meetings, I submitted myself to Dr. Dufresne as a son in the faith. Dr. Dufresne confirmed that God had already spoken to him to be a father to me. I now had a spiritual father. My life and ministry have never been the same. There was an immediate sense of security and a settling in my spirit that I was in the right place now as Dr. Dufresne became my spiritual father. I now had the covering that I needed. I was no longer fatherless.

Scripture indicates that men throughout history have been anointed to stand as spiritual fathers. These men do not take the place of God, but they are used by God to father those in the body of Christ. God is the God of order. A spiritual father is often used to establish divine order over a period of time. Paul wrote, *"...And the rest will I set in order when I come."* (1 Corinthians 11:34) Paul indicated that, as a spiritual father, he had the authority to set things in divine order. Notice that he would set *"the rest"* in order. Some order had already been established in the church at Corinth, but a spiritual father was required to order the remaining

> *"A true spiritual father is not one who comes to overrun the authority of a minister or the personal decisions of a sheep."*

areas. That was my situation in 1994. An impartation through my spiritual father equipped me to make the necessary adjustments in my life and in my ministry. The area in my life that had been wanting was now filled. The fathered minister and believer will always experience more than ever possible had they chosen to be fatherless.

A true spiritual father is not one who comes to overrun the authority of a minister or the personal decisions of a sheep. A father is one who offers a spiritually mature view and counsels a son or daughter toward order. True spiritual fathers come to help, not dominate. (2 Corinthians 1:24)

I pray this book will cause faith to grow in your heart concerning this valuable gift that God has given His church, the spiritual father.

Spiritual 1 Fathers

Scripture indicates there were a number of men who stood as spiritual fathers to those doing the work of God's kingdom. Paul makes mention of his role as a spiritual father to those in the church at Corinth.

> **For though ye have ten thousand instructors in Christ, <u>yet have ye not many fathers: for in Christ Jesus I have begotten you through the gospel.</u>** *(1 Corinthians 4:15)*

One translation of this passage says *"but you don't have many spiritual fathers."* Men throughout history have been anointed to stand as spiritual fathers. These men do not take the place of God, but they are used by God to father those in the body of Christ. For the local church sheep, this father is the pastor. For a minister, this father should be a more seasoned minister. This relationship is intended to be one of loyal dedication for both parties. The *Message Paraphrase* says of First Corinthians 4:15...

> **There are a lot of people around who can't wait to tell you what you've done wrong, <u>but</u>**

***there aren't many fathers willing to take the
time and effort to help you grow up...***

There are many anointed ministers, but not all are fathers.
There are some Bible scholars, but not many fathers who will
take the time to field your "hard to answer" questions. There are
many articulate television ministers, but not many fathers who are
willing to be awakened in the night to pray for you and your family.
There are many great expounders of the scriptures, but not many
fathers who will see you through to the end. The question we
must all be willing to answer is this, "Do I have a father?"

**A father will present the life-giving Word of God and
keep us mindful of its value.** In turn, we will become established
in that truth. Many may present this truth, but are they willing to
stay in contact and keep you mindful of it in your time of need? (2
Peter 1:12)

Spiritual fathers do not abandon their children! It is
obvious from the high number of single parent homes that many
natural fathers have abandoned their role as protector. Spiritual
fathers can follow this same destructive pattern. (Isaiah 56:10-11
and John 10:12)

**A spiritual father offers protection for the family in a
variety of ways.** Protection may come as a father confronts
those with improper motives, warns of possible danger, or covers

his children with prayer. True fathers stand boldly in the face of persecution and affliction because they are willing to lay down their life for the family. (John 10:11) Every family needs a protector.

In First Samuel 12:10, the children of Israel cried out, *"...We have sinned, because we have forsaken the LORD, and have served Baalim and Ashtaroth: but now deliver us out of the hand of our enemies, and we will serve thee."* God responded by placing them under the caring oversight of a spiritual father. (1 Samuel 12:10-11) The result of this fathered life was safety. Just as the presence of a natural father evokes security in the hearts of his natural children, the same is true for a spiritual father and his spiritual children. The fatherless must constantly guard against the swindlers and gamblers who target the fatherless family. The presence of a father, however, will deter such drifters by his mere presence.

> *"Just as the presence of a natural father evokes security in the hearts of his natural children, the same is true for a spiritual father and his spiritual children."*

True spiritual fathers understand timing. In Acts 15:37-38, Paul's refusal to take John Mark on the mission trip was not a rejection of John Mark. Paul understood that John Mark was not quite ready for such a journey and what would be required of him. By his second letter to Timothy, Paul called for John Mark, saying, *"he is profitable to me for the ministry."* John Mark was now ready. (2 Timothy 4:11) The right timing of a thing is important. (Ecclesiastes 8:5b-6)

Unfortunately, not everyone understands timing. One young man came after a service and asked me to lay hands on him because he was going to Australia as a missionary. I refused. (1 Timothy 5:22) I barely knew him. He had rarely come to our church services. I could not possibly endorse a call that I did not know was genuine! Although some have legitimate calls of God on their lives, they fail to realize there is a season of training before being launched into ministry.

> *Now I say, That the heir, as long as he is a child, differeth nothing from a servant, though he be lord of all; But is under tutors and governors until the time appointed of the father. (Galatians 4:1-2)*

Although this heir was *"lord of all"* he continued to live a life that *"differeth nothing from a servant."* It was only as the heir allowed himself to be matured through proper training and mentoring that he walked in the fulness of his inheritance. Notice the length of this training period, *"...until the time appointed of the father."* Another translation says, *"... until the date fixed by his father."* It was not just any father that set the duration of this training, it was specifically set by *"his"* father, the father assigned by God. The word "father" in this verse is the same Greek word translated "father" in First Corinthians 4:15 when discussing the spiritual father. Spiritual fathers understand the right timing of a thing.

As a true father, you are not only imparting the Word that you minister, but a portion of yourself. *Thayer's Greek Definitions* says that a *father* is "one who has infused his own spirit into others." Every person you allow to speak in your pulpit will leave a deposit of something. Paul said, *"I long to see you that I may impart..."* Something was transmitted.

> *So being affectionately desirous of you, we were willing to have imparted unto you, not the gospel of God only, <u>but also our own souls</u>, because ye were dear unto us.*
> *(1 Thessalonians 2:8)*

As members of a biological family, there is DNA that can be found in the father and his children. Could you find the spiritual DNA of any father in your spiritual make up?

Fathers have the ability to bless and impart. It was Timothy's spiritual father, Paul, who was responsible for the *"...gift of God, which is in thee (Timothy) by the putting on of my (Paul's) hands."* (2 Timothy 1:6) Paul was not the source of this impartation, but he was the one used by the Father to transmit this gift to his son. Believers must realize it is through the hands of a father that God releases His blessing.

True spiritual fathers have proven fruit. (Proverbs 25:14) Fruit in their ministry, fruit in their family, and fruit among their spiritual children. Many begin with a splash, but sink after a season. True fathers continue to produce great yields of fruit throughout their latter years. Such are to be followed. (Psalm 92:13-14)

As a seasoned minister, a spiritual father can help a believer avoid many of the pitfalls the enemy has to offer. The father has been there. He can use his experiences, both positive and negative, to direct his children toward an easier path if they choose to follow. Sons and daughters will not "pioneer" many areas of life and ministry because the father has already done so for them. (Hebrews 6:11-12)

It is a father who has been willing to be corrected by the Father and his spiritual father so that he is now qualified to assist in the restoration of those who have fallen. (Galatians 6:1 AMP) Not only can this type of spiritual father bring restoration to one who has been overtaken, but a real spiritual father will correct and reprove. He is not

> *"...it is through the hands of a father that God releases His blessing."*

intimidated to speak strongly, even when the correction is difficult to voice. If such counsel is heeded, the anointing on your life can increase and become stronger. **It is a great joy for a father to see this type of fruit in his children.** (3 John 1:4 AMP) Real spiritual fathers bring correction only when necessary. No one enjoys having to correct their children, but such correction is necessary to avoid future problems. This is part of the training process. When training children one must help direct their giftings by telling them what is appropriate and inappropriate. True fathers answer that call. (Proverbs 22:6 AMP)

Training spiritual children is not merely done by word, it is done by deed. Mentoring is a lifestyle. A father must lead his children by example. I have a spiritual father whose example I follow. I listen to his words and follow his advise. I also am a father with children following me. It is by my following that I give others a pattern to follow. (1 Corinthians 11:1) Some want children, but they are unwilling to follow.

> *Those things, which ye have both <u>learned, and received, and heard, and seen in me, do</u>: and the God of peace shall be with you. (Philippians 4:9)*

Natural Families and Spiritual Families

There has been considerable research about children who do not have a father in the home. Most agree it is best to have a father in the home of a biological family, but what about the "fatherless" spiritual family?

Knowing there are patterns in the natural that apply to the spirit, it is obvious that God has always intended for a man to act as a spiritual covering for His children. There are clear parallels between the biological family and the spiritual family. (1 Corinthians 15:46) Scripture indicates it is not only biological children who are to be taught of the Lord, but spiritual children as well.

> *And __all of your [spiritual] children shall be disciples [taught by the Lord and obedient to His will]__, and great shall be the peace and undisturbed composure of your children.*
> *(Isaiah 54:13 AMP)*

Spiritual children are to become disciples, not converts only. Conversion is the first step to discipleship, but it is not the finished product. A child who is birthed into a natural family has much to learn before being sent out on their own. The same is true of the believer. The result of being fathered is great "peace and undisturbed composure." Peace and composure are not possible without the instruction and caring guidance of a father. (Proverbs 1:8, 3:12)

We have all seen children who run a home. Getting their way through manipulation and tantrums, they believe the end justifies the means. Is it possible that these same types of relations exist in the church? There are spiritual children who threaten abandonment if they do not get their way. Some will even try to gain the favor of their spiritual father through manipulation and dissimilation. Although these are not the tantrums of a three year old, they are viewed as such by God. Such children need scriptural discipline. Paul said we ought to know how to *behave* in the house of God. (1 Timothy 3:15)

The Fatherless

The fatherless are spiritual orphans. They may be a sheep with no shepherd or a minister with an illegitimate ministry. Regardless, any inheritance from a father is withheld. Either there is no father wanted or no father available. There will always be lack where there is no spiritual father.

The fatherless are lacking because there is no father to help establish the family and supply those needs. (Romans 1:11-12) A fathering relationship requires a commitment from both parties to see the process through to the end. Time, patience, effort, and change are essential to the success of this relationship. Some make the mistake of rejecting their spiritual father before he has supplied these needs. (1 Thessalonians 3:10) Even Jesus was under training from the Heavenly Father for 30 years prior to His entrance into full time ministry. (Luke 3:23) He had taken time to be fully equipped.

> *"There will always be lack where there is no spiritual father."*

Elisha was another who was unwilling to be fatherless. We see throughout his relationship with Elijah that he refused to leave his spiritual father. Elisha's heart was to stay close to his spiritual father to be a help and a blessing. (2 Kings 2:1-8) Some recognize, in part, what it takes to move with the things of God. They are not willing, however, to pay the price. The sons of the prophets viewed the passing of an anointing from Elijah to Elisha, but they did so from *"afar off."* (2 Kings 2:7) A fathering relationship cannot take place from "afar off." Some things that are needful to be learned from a spiritual father will have to be *caught*, not just taught. You will need to be *there* with them for that to take place.

True Sons and Daughters

True children love their father. They understand that their father's many years of work is an investment in their future. They would never betray that trust and faithfully commit to his success. False children have no real heart for their father. They are willing to use the notoriety and "connections" of the father to help spring board themselves and their ministries into prominence. They are not willing to serve in that which is another man's yet want others to faithfully serve them. (Luke 16:10-12) They will take advantage of their father's loyalty and abandon him when they feel it is time to make it on their own.

A true son or daughter will take the time to be around their father and receive the impartations necessary to finish their course. Their agenda takes second place to that of their father. False sons and daughters are more interested in their activities than sitting under their man of God. Their desire is to receive an offering instead of sowing into one. They sacrifice a divine endowment for personal gain.

True sons and daughters do not abandon their fathers. (2 Kings 2:6) Although there will be opportunities to do so, true spiritual children know the value of staying close and walking in the steps of their father. It is a father who sets the path that is easy for the children to follow. False children are willing to stray from their father if a different path will lead to a quicker promotion. They fail to realize that such promotion is short lived.

> *I desired Titus, and with him I sent a brother.*
> *Did Titus make a gain of you?* <u>*walked we*</u>
> <u>*not in the same spirit?*</u> <u>*walked we not in the*</u>
> <u>*same steps?*</u> *(2 Corinthians 12:18)*

I recall a time when my spiritual father was in a city about 100 miles from my home. I had been busy with the activities of the day and had wavered on attending. As the time for the meeting grew closer, the Spirit of God prompted me to be in the service that evening. I called a son in the faith and we traveled to the meeting. We entered late and the service had already begun. As we sat in the back of the sanctuary, I watched as my spiritual father began ministering through the laying on of hands. As I watched, God began to deal with me about the way I ministered

> *"True spiritual children communicate often concerning situations and early when difficult decisions must be made. "*

during ministry time. He used my father's example to point out some of the mistakes I had been making. I not only took notes that evening with my pen, but with my eyes. The adjustments made from that meeting have greatly blessed me and the sons and daughters under my care. Had I missed that meeting, I would have missed a vital lesson that helped equip me for the future. I had to be around my father to walk in *those* steps.

True sons and daughters do not have hidden motives. The actions of true sons and daughters relay what is in their heart. False sons and daughters, on the other hand, offer lip service. They profess to honor their father, but demonstrate their true attitude when correction comes. They are only transparent when it will benefit their progress. If such transparency will derail their plans for advancement, they remain quiet and internally frustrated.

True spiritual children communicate with their fathers. True spiritual children communicate often concerning situations and early when difficult decisions must be made. They do not hide problems from their father in hopes he will not find out about them. They know that the best way to right a wrong is by allowing direction from the voice of a father. False sons and daughters hide the truth. They communicate their praise reports yet forget to mention their challenges. They are concerned that a bad report will hinder their position as a son or daughter. They never understand that true spiritual fathers are not only interested in cheering over your triumphs, but helping you overcome your difficulties.

True sons and daughters are willing to take responsibility for their position in the family. True sons and daughters know there is great accountability that comes with being a son or daughter. (Luke 12:48b) When guidance comes, they know their father is using his experience to save them from disaster. True sons and daughters are grateful for that! False children resent correction and guidance when it does not fit with their agenda. They will heed the counsel of a father in the "little matters" yet reject advice that will short-circuit their plans for popularity. They resent his loving attempts to steer them from danger.

Spiritual fathers will need the help of their sons and daughters to fulfill their callings. (2 Timothy 4:11) True sons and daughters offer that help. They will help with their anointings, with their prayers, and with their finances. They are unwilling to see their father struggle. They know that they are in a covenant relationship where they are to offer their strength. They do not forget all the times that their father has helped them. False sons and daughters seem to be forgetful. Forgetful of the father's seed

> *"True sons and daughters...help with their anointings, with their prayers, and with their finances. They are unwilling to see their father struggle."*

sown, forgetful of the father's prayers, and forgetful of who launched them into the ministry. In a father's greatest time of need, false children will abandon him. (2 Timothy 4:10)

I have one spiritual son who is very experienced at travel. It is a strength which he possesses. He has said to me, *"As long as I am in the earth I will help with your travel arrangements." "I'll help you." "It is not a problem." "I'll take care of it."* He does so because he is a true son helping his father.

Some Examples of True Spiritual Sons

Elisha, a son of Elijah

Elisha was known as a servant. (2 Kings 3:11) His heart was not for his upcoming ministry, but for that of his father. Had he been in the modern day church, many would call him a *"Yes Man."* Others would criticize him for being a puppet, cowering to the will of another. People tend to be jealous of those who have paid a price they are unwilling to pay.

Elisha understood that his place was with the one who had invested so much into his life. Elisha was unwilling to leave his man of God though it would demand effort and change to stay close. (2 Kings 2:1-8) In Second Kings 2:9-10, Elijah was about to leave the earth and an anointing was about to be passed. Elijah asked Elisha what it was that he desired. Elijah did not ask the sons of the prophets what they wanted. They loved God. They studied

> *"People tend to be jealous of those who have paid a price they are unwilling to pay."*

the writings. Elijah was not, however, their father. Many want an impartation from a father that is reserved for the sons and daughters of that father. They want it, but they will not commit to being fathered.

Notice Elisha's response when his father was taken. *"...My father, my father, the chariot of Israel, and the horsemen thereof. And he saw him no more: and he took hold of his own clothes, and rent them in two pieces."* (2 Kings 2:11-12) Elisha was sad to see his father leave. His heart was not for what his father could give him. His heart was for his father.

Did Elisha receive the request made of his father?

> ***He took up also the mantle of Elijah that fell from him, and went back, and stood by the bank of Jordan; And he took the mantle of Elijah that fell from him, and smote the waters, and said, Where is the LORD God of Elijah? and when he also had smitten the waters, they parted hither and thither: and Elisha went over. (2 Kings 2:13-14)***

How did Elisha know how to smite the waters of the Jordan? He took the time to be around his father and follow in his steps. How did Elisha get the same spirit as his father? He took the time to receive the impartation that was needed to fulfill his destiny.

How will you receive what is needed? By taking the time to be around your spiritual father and allowing him to father you. I have spent time and thousands of dollars to be around my spiritual father. It has been a privilege. It has been worth every cent. I have received

> *"Elisha was sad to see his father leave."*

impartations by teachings, by laying on of hands, and through conversations. All by being around my spiritual dad.

Timothy, a son of Paul

Timothy's focus was the work of his father. He was not overly interested in the recognition of his ministry or gifting. His heart was to serve his father, Paul, as a son in the gospel. When you saw Timothy, you saw his father. He was a "chip off the old block." Certainly there were differences between Paul and Timothy, but the similarities were unquestionable. (Philippians 2:19-24)

True children will always have some traits of their father. It is a compliment to the true son or daughter to be told of such similarities. The false, however, despise such comparisons. They thrive on compliments of their uniqueness and independence. Their desire is to be *self* made and for those around them to notice *their* hard work. They never grasp the concept that two are better than one. (Ecclesiastes 4:9, 12b)

Titus, a son of Paul

Titus was a man of the same faith as his father. (Titus 1:4-5) He could be trusted to do what his father had appointed. Paul did not have to wonder if Titus was heeding his instruction. He knew that as a true son, Titus would honor his words.

Paul had such great confidence in Titus because he knew of his character. Paul knew how Titus would conduct himself. Just like his father! (2 Corinthians 12:17-19) Titus had the same spirit as Paul due to the impartations he had received through the years. He walked in the same steps because he had watched his father in a number of difficult settings. Sons and daughters who take the time to be around their father are a great source of security for their father. The father knows that they will not leave a bad deposit in the people to whom they have been sent. False children, on the other hand, can leave a father guessing, *"What next?"*

Some Examples of False Spiritual Sons

Ham, a false son of Noah

Ham became aware of a mistake his father had made. What would he do with this information? Would he help his father or expose his nakedness? He chose to expose. He spread the mistake of his father to others while the true sons chose to help their father in his time of need. Ham had forgotten that his deliverance from the flood was due to his father. Shem and Japeth did not forget that fact. Shem and Japeth covered their father's nakedness without focusing on it. Where are the Shems and Japeths of the modern church? "Hams" work to highly perfect the art of gossip and talebearing, but true spiritual children always believe the best and are slow to speak. (Genesis 9:18-27) The father was wrong for being drunk and naked, but the son was more wrong for spreading the father's shortcomings

> *"Hams work to highly perfect the art of gossip and talebearing, but true spiritual children always believe the best and are slow to speak."*

throughout the community. Mistakes must be addressed, but it is the spiritual who are to restore the fallen. (Galatians 6:1) Gossips and talebearers prove by their actions that they are neither spiritual nor qualified to restore.

Esau, a false son of Isaac

Esau was the firstborn, but did not understand the importance of his position in the family. His hunger motivated him to forfeit his rightful inheritance. When driven by his flesh, his birthright meant very little. (Genesis 25:29-34) Believers abandon their inheritance today in much the same way. It may not be the physical hunger mentioned here, but it is none the less damaging. It may be the hunger for promotion, or the hunger for position, the hunger for a better job, or the hunger for money that causes them to forfeit their inheritance. They allow their flesh and unrenewed mind to dictate their decisions. It is only as time passes that they regret what they have foolishly squandered. What is lost cannot always be regained. (Hebrews 12:16-17)

Absalom, a false son of David

Absalom's sister Tamar was raped by her half brother, Amnon. (2 Samuel 13:1-29) Not being pleased with King David's (his father's) response to this crime, Absalom took matters into his own hands and murdered Amnon. After the murder, Absalom fled, but later returned at the urging of his father. While away, however, Absalom plotted revenge against his father. Absalom intended to undermine the intentions of his father by lying to the people. He hoped to draw away disciples to himself in an attempt to take the kingdom from his father. (2 Samuel 15:2-6) Although he saw limited success in his early ventures, he eventually met the fate of many false sons in scripture.

> *And Absalom met the servants of David. And Absalom rode upon a mule, and the mule went under the thick boughs of a great oak, and his head caught hold of the oak, and he was taken up between the heaven and the earth; and the mule that was under him went away.* <u>*And a certain man saw it, and told*</u>

Joab, and said, Behold, I saw Absalom
hanged in an oak. *(2 Samuel 18:9-10)*

Then said Joab, I may not tarry thus with
thee. And he took three darts in his hand,
and thrust them through the heart of
Absalom, while he was yet alive in the midst
of the oak. And ten young men that bare
Joab's armour compassed about and smote
Absalom, and slew him.
(2 Samuel 18:14-15)

False sons and daughters may not realize it, but they often take the same path as Absalom. It is an all too familiar scenario. The spiritual father makes a decision with which they do not agree. They, in turn, choose to be offended over that decision. They seek out others to support their offense. They begin to drop hints in an effort to find other false children. (The offended always seem to find one another.) These pockets of disunity will then see if they have enough support to call for a mutiny. *"He's in error!"* or *"Well, guess what I heard..."* are sometimes the slogans for their campaigns. If successful, they attempt to disconnect as many children from their father as possible through lies and manipulation. If unsuccessful, they will disconnect themselves. They have never taken the time to see that such politicking always ends in death. Death in their finances, death in their spiritual lives, death in their revelation from the Word of God, and sometimes physical death.

Being Properly Connected

Divine Connection

It is through divine connections that great blessings manifest in a person's life. Those who choose to stay planted in a fathering relationship are those who flourish. (Psalm 92:13) The will of God is to show Himself benevolent to all who love Him, but it is through divine connections that the blessings of God must flow. It is not always a lack of anointing that causes little manifestation of God's power, it is a lack of being properly connected.

> *__From whom the whole body fitly joined together and compacted by that which every joint supplieth, according to the effectual working in the measure of every part,...__*
> *(Ephesians 4:16)*

> *And not holding the Head, __from which all the body by joints and bands having nourishment ministered, and knit together, increaseth with the increase of God.__*
> *(Colossians 2:19)*

Every believer has a specific part to play and a specific connection that is needed. There is no part in the Body of Christ that is insignificant. When a believer chooses not to do their part or to not be properly connected, another is effected. When one disconnects, they impact those to whom they were once connected. Just as there is no part of the human body that can exist on its own ability, there is no part of His body that can do so. God does not endorse spiritual lone rangers.

The divinely connected, know their identity and who they are. This takes place because there is a lineage of faith in their spiritual family tree. When divinely connected, believers fulfill their purpose and stay on course. Certainly, there are connections within the local church body, but the true order of God's kingdom has always been father to son.

The passing of the blessing and inheritance is from father to son. A father-son relationship is the divine order needed by God to pass on these anointings. Without this connection there is no passing of anointings or true basis of spiritual authority. This divine

> *"Many want the benefits of being fathered, but fear the accountability."*

connection is between a father and his children, not children and an organization. If there were no father-son relationships, who would be passing on an inheritance? An organization? Without divine connections, the anointings of great men and women of God would be lost when they leave the earth. It is through the father-son relationship that an inheritance is passed to the next generation of believers. Many miss out on an inheritance because they are fatherless.

God always intended for a spiritual covering to be over His family. God's first man, Adam, was properly covered.

> *Which was the son of Enos, which was the son of Seth, which was the son of __Adam,__ __which was the son of God.__ (Luke 3:38)*

Not even Jesus stepped into ministry until endorsed by His Father. (Mark 1:11-14) If Jesus did not minister until being endorsed, do we have the freedom to do so before a spiritual father has endorsed us? Gifts, skills, talents, and abilities mean nothing until a father voices his approval and offers a pattern to follow. (John 5:19)

Many want the benefits of being fathered, but fear the accountability. Others want an inheritance from a rich spiritual lineage, yet despise the thought of submitting to anyone but themselves. Although the stability of being fathered is desirable, some fail to overcome the obstacles that prevent this connection.

Consumed with personal schedules, they disregard the command to come together and sit under their father. These are perimeter people. Their lives are characterized by the ups and downs of the disconnected. They are high maintenance and low output. They are the Lots of the modern church. Lot abandoned his man of God over cattle. (Genesis 13:5-6, 8, 11) He chose physical substance over spiritual supply.

> *"Lot abandoned his man of God over cattle. He chose physical substance over spiritual supply."*

His life and that of his family plummets into disaster after this decision. His daughters are offered to appease the lusts of wicked men. His wife dies due to her refusal to reject the sins of Sodom. Lot's own daughters sleep with him in an effort to preserve his lineage. It is sad how some will attempt to counterfeit a lineage after abandoning the lineage established by God. (Genesis 19:8, 26, 30-38)

God also knows that some do not take correction easily. He knows that some view correction as a personal attack, rather than the guiding hand of a loving father. God knows the temptation to disconnect and sulk, but implores the corrected against such a mistake. It is only through correction that appropriate adjustments can take place. It is through correction that misplaced effort can be properly placed. It is through correction that a sheep fold is kept in divine order. It is through correction that wrongs can be made right. Those who leave their place after correction merely compound their problems by committing another wrong. (Ecclesiastes 10:4)

Some believers are led astray by those who profess to have their best interests in mind. It is amazing how often there is a *"who."* (Galatians 5:7-9) These deceived souls become dull to the fact that the evil communications of this *"who"* have infected their scriptural behavior. (1 Corinthians 15:33) The *"persuaded"* begin to believe they would be better off as a spiritual orphan. They fall prey to the speeches about spiritual freedom and the false ads of being held back by a father. The *"who"* are spiritual lobbyists. Their platform is desertion, their target audience is the fathered, and their campaign is energized by past offenses.

Being Properly Connected Provides Covering

> ***Behold, how good and how pleasant it is for brethren to dwell together in unity!*** <u>***It is like the precious ointment upon the head, that ran down upon the beard, even Aaron's beard: that went down to the skirts of his garments;***</u> ***As the dew of Hermon, and as the dew that descended upon the mountains of Zion: for there the LORD commanded the blessing, even life for evermore.***
> ***(Psalm 133:1-3)***

The anointing always flows downward from head to toe. Under the new covenant, it is the flow of a father-son relationship that provides this anointing. A fathering relationship is a covenant relationship. It is more than attending a church or going to a meeting. It is more than hearing a preacher or being invited to the back room. It is more than giving your time and money. It is more than being on staff or in an organization. It is a relationship where you commit yourself to the success of your father and he commits to yours.

I remember covenanting myself to my spiritual father during a luncheon, years ago. As I mentioned in the introduction, God brought my spiritual father into my life to help supply what was *lacking* in my ministry and church. While eating lunch during those meetings, I mentioned that I felt God was leading me to be a spiritual son to him. He responded by saying that God had already confirmed he was to be my spiritual father. He then handed me his cell phone number and encouraged me to call whenever I needed him. He then said, *"Of course you understand that this means I can call you whenever I need you."* I responded, *"Yes sir, I understand covenant."* Later, during those same meetings, he came over to where I was sitting, laid his hands on

> *"It is only by properly placing ourselves under the care of a father that the impartations needed to finish our course are received."*

me, pulled me close to him, and said, *"What I have, let go into this man."* I immediately noticed spiritual things on the inside of me coming to a new level of intensity. The gifts of the Spirit and my discernment also came to a new level. I received an impartation.

Although I received an impartation during that first meeting, there are some impartations that do not come until further in the fathering relationship. Impatient sons run off after receiving an initial impartation thinking they have been *fully equipped*. They do not take the time to be fully endued because their flesh pressures them to "make a name" for themselves. Such behavior leads to limited impact. It is through long lasting, covenant relationships that anointings are passed from generation to generation in the spiritual family. It is only by properly placing ourselves under the care of a father that the impartations needed to finish our course are received. Fathers are older and more seasoned in their callings and giftings. They have been proven and have established character and integrity. Fathers go before us so that we can follow in their footsteps. They have been where we need to go.

The Connection of Sons and Daughters

And it shall come to pass in the last days, saith God, I will pour out of my Spirit upon all flesh: and your sons and your daughters shall prophesy, and your young men shall see visions, and your old men shall dream dreams: (Acts 2:17)

The *first message* of Pentecost dealt with being properly connected. The group said to be spearheading the supernatural in the end times will be the sons and daughters, not the fatherless. The Spirit is being poured out on all flesh, but all flesh will not be moving in what is available. It is the sons and daughters who know how to flow with the Holy Ghost and fulfill their ministries. Many operate in the gifts of the Spirit, but are they fathered?

> ...***Is Saul also among the prophets? And one of the same place answered and said, But who is their father?*** *(1 Samuel 10:5-12)*

There was prophesying in this Old Testament meeting, but those who heard it asked, *"Who is their father?"* The people wanted to know who was the covering for this supernatural display. They wanted to know if this activity was properly sanctioned. The church will often allow anyone to come in and move in the gifts of the Spirit, but the discerning want to know to whom they are accountable.

Many years ago I met a talented young lady who was singing in a meeting where I had been invited to minister. A pastor friend encouraged me to have her to my church so I asked if she had any available dates. After setting a date I asked about her pastor. She stuttered and stammered before finally admitting that she was "between"

"Who is their father?"

pastors. She was uncovered! She had no father! I had just invited an unaccountable singer into my fold! I had sworn to my own hurt. I explained that I would keep my word, but had I known she was *shepherdless* I would never have invited her to minister. That will not happen again! I now ask about their pastor before asking to see their date book. The talented are a dime a dozen, but the accountable are more precious than gold.

Recovering Lost Axe Heads

A Father, His Son, and a Lost Axe Head

And the sons of the prophets said unto Elisha, Behold now, the place where we dwell with thee is too strait for us. Let us go, we pray thee, unto Jordan, and take thence every man a beam, and let us make us a place there, where we may dwell. And he answered, Go ye. And one said, Be content, I pray thee, and go with thy servants. And he answered, I will go. So he went with them. <u>And when they came to Jordan, they cut down wood. But as one was felling a beam, the axe head fell into the water: and he cried, and said, Alas, master! for it was borrowed. And the man of God said, Where fell it? And he shewed him the place. And he cut down a stick, and cast it in thither; and the iron did swim. Therefore said he, Take it up to thee. And he</u>

put out his hand, and took it.
(2 Kings 6:1-7)

That axe head was vitally needed by the young prophet. It would have been virtually impossible to accomplish his task without that important piece of equipment. He wisely asked his father to help retrieve what had been lost.

This dilemma in the natural underlies a spiritual principle. A son or daughter needs special equipment to fulfill their call. This equipment can be lost or lie dormant. A father helps retrieve such equipment. A son or daughter can be doing their best to fulfill a call in the local church or in the fields of the world, but without the proper materials their fruit is limited at best. There is a dull "thud" in their efforts. A father can hear a spiritual "thud" and help find the missing axe head. Fathers get to the cause of missing or dormant equipment and help restore what is needed. Cutting down a tree without an axe head requires

> *"Fathers get to the cause of missing or dormant equipment and help restore what is needed."*

quite a bit of work. Unfortunately, that is the situation of many in the local church and in full time ministry today. They are fatherless, they have lost their axe head, and they are tirelessly attempting to do their part for the kingdom. (Ecclesiastes 10:10) They lack the accuracy and equipment to get the job done with efficiency and ease. For them it is neither light nor easy. (Matthew 11:30)

Accuracy is a must for successful ministry. Without the proper equipment, accuracy is not possible. Without a spiritual father, the proper equipment will not be retrieved. Without a spiritual father, accuracy in ministry is not attainable. That is why the fatherless are so often weak, they faint, or they die prematurely. (1 Corinthians 11:29-30) Their lack of accuracy has led to the wearing out of their bodies and, in some cases, an early grave. There is no divine promotion for the

> *"There is no divine promotion for the fatherless."*

fatherless. Their refusal to sow faithfulness into that which is another's has doomed their aspirations of that which is their own. (Luke 16:10-12) Their desire for the submission of others is met by the seeds of unfaithfulness they have sown in times past. *"Thud."* Their unwillingness to serve another has led to their stewardship of a "ministry" of dried, dead bones. *"Thud."* The more they have pursued independence, without accountability, the more they have stripped themselves of authority. Their ministries are characterized by inaccuracy.

It is a father who will guide the way to a long and successful ministry in the earth. When a father is speaking, it is the voice of past generations offering their counsel. When a father is speaking, it is not merely the outpouring of their thirty or forty years of ministry experience. It is a deluge of their father's, and their father's, and their father's experiences and impartations that speak. A wise son or daughter will choose to sit at the feet of a father who is bringing forth such precious revelation. During these intimate times a father can impart the knowledge of past generations to his children. It is in these times that keys for longevity in life and ministry are offered to the true sons and daughters. Only the foolish would be busy about the cares of their own ministry during such times. (Luke 10:38-42)

Below are some of the keys that I have been so honored to receive as I sat at the feet of my father...

Stay in Your Office of Ministry or Get in the Right One.

I have met ministers over the years who cannot seem to find their place in the Body of Christ. One year they are a pastor, the next an evangelist, the third a Bible school teacher, and the fourth a pastor again. What is their office? Where is their place? What is their identity? How can one possibly be effective when they do not stay rooted in the office to which they have been called? (1 Corinthians 12:28-30)

Don't Take Every Invitation.

Every invitation to minister is not a divine invitation. Often times believers view a minister's full itinerary as a sign of God's approval. This is not always the case. A minister can fill a schedule through divine connections or by the sweat of the brow. Those who consistently take invitations that are not divinely orchestrated squander the anointing on their life and wear themselves out physically. God always supplies His ability for those things He has called us to do. If a minister has filled his calendar with meetings by passing out cards or politicking he is left to his own ability. Longevity in ministry is significantly increased for those who rely on *His* ability and take only those meetings that are in *His* will.

Go Where Your Favor is and Where You are Honored.

Too often believers attend a meeting expecting a man or woman of God to *wow* them with their gifting. Usually these same people leave saying, *"They sure weren't very anointed tonight."* That is no surprise. The minister had to ride all day in the cramped coach section of a flight and endured three layovers because the church wanted the cheapest fare. They then placed the man of God in a dilapidated hotel across town because the board did not want to seem wasteful. They thought the minister should be able to arrive in town by 4:00 PM and be prepared to minister that evening by 7:00 PM in the fullness of the Spirit. Finally

> *"Those who consistently take invitations that are not divinely orchestrated squander the anointing on their life and wear themselves out physically."*

at the service, the people thought the success or failure of the meeting was based solely on the one ministering. How can a minister possibly be at his best after such a day? I understand that we are people of faith, but what ever happened to honoring the gift in the minister?

> *And it fell on a day, that Elisha passed to Shunem, where was a great woman; and she constrained him to eat bread. And so it was, that as oft as he passed by, he turned in thither to eat bread.* <u>*And she said unto her husband, Behold now, I perceive that this is an holy man of God, which passeth by us continually. Let us make a little chamber, I pray thee, on the wall; and let us set for him there a bed, and a table, and a stool, and a candlestick: and it shall be, when he cometh to us, that he shall turn in thither. And it fell on a day, that he came thither, and he turned into the chamber, and lay there.*</u>
> *(2 Kings 4:8-11)*

The Shunammite woman mentioned in this passage understood more about honoring the gift than most new covenant believers and churches. She made a special room for the man of God when he was in town. A place to rest and refresh himself after a long day of traveling. Her reward for this honor was the desire of her heart, a son. (2 Kings 4:12-17) Why do we so rarely see God moving through His ministers in this same fashion today? Most in the modern church do not understand how to show the proper honor to a man or woman of God. What about bringing him in a day early to rest and be refreshed before imparting to the sheep? What about teaching the people that there is an expectancy needed by those attending the meetings? (Acts 3:5) Why not place the minister in one of the nicest rooms in your city? Is the money more important than the impartation he brings to your congregation? Sadly, many ministers go back to churches where they are run through the wringer, much like the scenario described earlier. They receive very little honor from those to whom they are ministering. A continued lifestyle of this sort will eventually shorten their ministry.

> *"Most in the modern church do not understand how to show the proper honor to a man or woman of God."*

Allow me to add this addendum when discussing honor for the man or woman of God. We are told in Matthew 28:19 and Mark 16:15 to go to all nations and share the gospel. Over time, however, those to whom we are sent should grow in their revelation of honor.

> *...but having hope, <u>when your faith is increased [through instruction], that we shall be enlarged by</u> you according to our rule abundantly, (2 Corinthians 10:15)*

A minister called to the mission fields and unreached people groups will have to teach about the principles of honor. It is not possible for a people group to walk in the blessings of a principle they are not taught. It is also impossible for a minister to *"come in the fulness of the blessing of the gospel of Christ"* if there is no honor for the ministry gift set in the midst of the congregation. (Romans 15:29) If there is no teaching on honor, there will be no honor. Notice the instruction offered by Jesus to His disciples about ministry and honor.

> ***And he said unto them, In what place soever ye enter into an house, there abide till ye depart from that place. <u>And whosoever shall not receive you, nor hear you, when ye depart thence, shake off the dust under your feet for a testimony against them.</u> Verily I say unto you, It shall be more tolerable for Sodom and Gomorrha in the day of judgment, than for that city. (Mark 6:10-11)***

A lack of honor is a bad testimony. Jesus noted a lack of honor as the reason for a poor meeting during His ministry in the earth. (Mark 6:1-6)

> ***But Jesus said unto them, A prophet is not <u>without honour</u>, but in his own country, and among his own kin, and in his own house. <u>And he could there do no mighty work</u>, save that he laid his hands upon a few sick folk, and healed them. And he marvelled because***

of their unbelief. And he went round about the villages, teaching. (Mark 6:4-6)

Jesus had a solution for the lack of honor shown in His hometown. *"And he went round about the villages, teaching."* The cure Jesus offered for a lack of honor was teaching on the subject. A younger minister may sometimes be in a church where honor is not understood or is not a priority. As a minister matures and becomes more seasoned, however, he should be very selective about his ministry engagements. Honor must be considered when making decisions about when and where to minister.

> *"Honor must be considered when making decisions about when and where to minister."*

Learn to Rest One Day a Week.

And on the seventh day God ended his work which he had made; and he rested on the seventh day from all his work which he had made. And God blessed the seventh day, and sanctified it: because that in it he had rested from all his work which God created and made. (Genesis 2:2-3)

God gave us an example to follow. Sometimes we become so busy with the activities of this life we forget to relax. We are recreated beings, but we live in physical bodies that need rest. Find out how you rest best. Regardless of your style, choose one day a week and learn to rest. It is not laziness, it is intelligence. It is unwise to preoccupy yourself with activities seven days a week, twenty-four hours a day. You must either make the decision to rest your body now or your body will make the decision to rest itself later.

Be Careful Who You Let Around You.

He that walketh with wise men shall be wise:
but a companion of fools shall be destroyed.
(Proverbs 13:20)

Those who are around you are allowed a place in your life. Their influence can be good or bad. The Word of God consistently warns of our companionships and those with whom we fellowship. Sometimes it can be a well meaning friend who unknowingly sways us from the path established by God. The influence of a staff member or a fellow believer may be just the thing that takes you out of God's will. Once off that path, it can take years to get back to where you belong. Time is precious. We do not need to waste it

> *"Sometimes it can be a well meaning friend who unknowingly sways us from the path established by God."*

by heeding the counsel of those who are not familiar with our calling nor God's will for our lives.

Teach Your Congregation to Reverence the Holy Ghost, Especially When He is Moving!

Quench not the Spirit.
(1 Thessalonians 5:19)

I recall a meeting I was hosting in a foreign country a number of years back. The Spirit of God was moving and there was a ministry line for those who needed healing in their bodies. As I was ministering, I heard an awful racket coming from the side of the meeting hall. As I turned, I saw that a group of people had taken out some food and begun eating. I abruptly stopped ministering and addressed those involved through my interpreter. I explained that such behavior grieved the Holy Spirit and the healing of those in the line could be hindered by such disrespect. Quickly, the food was put away and the service continued with many healings and miracles taking place. Some would say that such a rebuke was unwarranted, but those in the prayer line would not share that view. We must learn to reverence the Holy Spirit if we want Him to manifest on our behalf.

"We must learn to reverence the Holy Spirit if we want Him to manifest on our behalf."

Get to Know Your Pattern, What Works for You?

And when he had sent the multitudes away,
<u>*he went up into a mountain apart to pray:*</u>
and when the evening was come, he was there
alone. (Matthew 14:23)

And it came to pass in those days, that <u>he</u>
<u>*went out into a mountain to pray,*</u> *and*
continued all night in prayer to God.
(Luke 6:12)

During His earthly ministry, Jesus had patterns that worked best for Him. We see from scripture that He enjoyed going into the mountains to pray. Where do you like to pray? When do you like to pray? What works best for you? Some hear from God best when in their car. Others when in the shower. Some study better at night and others in the morning. What about ministry? What do you do to prepare yourself? Study, then pray about the message? Pray, then study the message out? Learn your pattern. God deals with people in patterns. If you learn your pattern and how God deals with you, it will be much easier to receive His counsel and direction for your personal life and ministry.

Be Willing to Change Everything and Anything if God Tells You to.

__Making the word of God of none effect__
__through your tradition,__ which ye have
delivered:... (Mark 7:13)

There is something more powerful than the Word of God.
Tradition. We must be willing to change anything that God wants
changed, including our traditions. Some argue, *"We have always
had three songs before service!"* Now God wants two. *"We
have always had a special meeting during June!"* Now God
says to move it to July. *"We have had
prayer on Monday night for sixteen
years!"* Now God wants it moved to
Sunday nights. We cannot allow
traditions or our routines to limit what
God wants to do in our lives. Spiritual
growth requires change. Some will not

> "There is
> something more
> powerful than
> the Word of
> God.
> Tradition."

allow God to do a new thing because change is often
uncomfortable. As a result, there is no spiritual growth. They will
continue circling the mountains of their parents, never realizing
that the cloud of His glory has long since moved. We must all
admit that if something is not growing, it is probably dead.

Stay with Your Spiritual Father!

*...and Elijah passed by him, and cast his
mantle upon him. And he left the oxen, and
ran after Elijah, and said, Let me, I pray thee,*

kiss my father and my mother, and then I will follow thee. And he said unto him, Go back again: for what have I done to thee? And he returned back from him, and <u>took a yoke of oxen, and slew them, and boiled their flesh with the instruments of the oxen, and gave unto the people, and they did eat.</u> Then he arose, and went after Elijah, and ministered unto him. (1 Kings 19:19b-21)

When Elisha made the decision to follow his spiritual father, he made certain there was nothing to which he could return. He had nothing to fall back on if this relationship did not work. He had already decided he was going to make it work!

As a spiritual son or daughter, there will be times when you may be tempted to leave your spiritual father. Elisha chose to make a "Me" thing a "We" thing. He knew that he needed his father if he was to fulfill the purpose for which he was born.

<u>Learn to Wait on the Lord.</u>

Or ministry, <u>let us wait on our ministering:</u> (Romans 12:7)

<u>But they that wait upon the LORD shall renew their strength; they shall mount up</u>

***with wings as eagles; they shall run, and not
be weary; and they shall walk, and not faint.
(Isaiah 40:31)***

We must wait long enough in the Lord's presence for an exchange to take place. The busyness of life will try to infringe on your time with the Father. If Satan cannot get you to sin, he will attempt to make you so busy that you neglect your time in God's presence. Either way, he has been successful in keeping you from a supply that will help you walk in your inheritance. The weary faint when pressure comes, but those who have spent time with their heavenly Father walk through the pressures of life. This is only possible for those who wait on the Lord.

Your Own Company

6

God has divinely appointed a place for each believer that is pleasing to Him. (1 Corinthians 12:18) A person may feel as if they fit best with a group to which they are not appointed. Don't leave your place! It is in your assigned post that the anointing and authority needed to carry out your purpose is located. There is great comfort in knowing that you are in the right company.

> *And being let go, <u>they went to their own company</u>, and reported all that the chief priests and elders had said unto them.*
> *(Acts 4:23)*

After being beaten and berated, Peter and John knew where they needed to go, their own company. Their company was made up of those with whom they shared a common bond. They were those with whom they had been placed by God. We must take the time to be with our own company. It is in these times that we can learn from those who are more seasoned. It is in these times that we learn how to function within our appointed place. It is in these times that a father can impart revelation that will help us more fully understand the ways of the Spirit. (2 Kings 2:14)

> ***Iron sharpeneth iron; so a man sharpeneth
> the countenance of his friend.***
> ***(Proverbs 27:17)***

Your father has been anointed to convey the blessing you need as a part of his company. As a member of the family, it is the place of the father to bless those in his spiritual lineage. Many times a father knows more about the anointing on your life than you do. It is by staying within your company and being around your father that he can perceive what you may need in a given situation. A child who consistently runs from company to company has allowed his father neither the time nor the opportunity to discern what is needed.

Honor the Gifts

...he led captivity captive, <u>and gave gifts unto</u>
<u>men</u>... And he gave some, apostles; and some,
prophets; and some, evangelists; and some,
pastors and teachers; <u>For the perfecting of</u>
<u>the saints</u>... (Ephesians 4:8b, 11-12a)

These gifts that we are to honor are the ministry gifts in men and women. God has placed these gifts over us to help in the things of the Spirit. For the sheep in the local church, it is the pastor who is your spiritual father. For others in ministry, it would be a more mature and seasoned minister. A spiritual father is not taking the place of your heavenly Father, nor competing with your biological father. God has ordained him to hold an important place in your life. Your recognition of him and the way you honor him will determine what you can receive from him and no more. Jesus described this type of honor in the account retold by Matthew.

He that receiveth you receiveth me, and he
that receiveth me receiveth him that sent me.

He that receiveth a prophet in the name of a prophet shall receive a prophet's reward; and he that receiveth a righteous man in the name of a righteous man shall receive a righteous man's reward. And whosoever shall give to drink unto one of these little ones a cup of cold water only in the name of a disciple, verily I say unto you, he shall in no wise lose his reward. (Matthew 10:40-42)

How you receive, or honor, is how you are rewarded. We often see three different men represented in these verses, but have we considered this may all be about the same person? When any ministry gift comes to minister, we must choose how we are going to receive the gift in that man or woman. These verses may refer to one person who has been received three different ways by three different people. One receives and honors him as a prophet. Another receives and honors him as a righteous man. The third receives and honors him as a disciple. They were all rewarded according to how they honored. Honor is more than an external behavior, it is a matter of attitude and respect. He who shows the most honor or respect can receive the most that ministry gift has to offer. This principle is clearly revealed in the ministry of Jesus.

> "Honor is more than an external behavior, it is a matter of attitude and respect."

And he went out from thence, and came into his own country; and his disciples follow him. And when the sabbath day was come, he began to teach in the synagogue: and many hearing him were astonished, saying, From whence hath this man these things? and what wisdom is this which is given unto him, that even such mighty works are wrought by his hands? Is not this the carpenter, the son of Mary, the brother of James, and Joses, and of Juda, and Simon? and are not his sisters here with us? And they were offended at him. But Jesus said unto them, A prophet is not without honour, but in his own country, and among his own kin, and in his own house. And he could there do no mighty work, save that he laid his hands upon a few sick folk, and healed them. And he marvelled because of their unbelief. And he went round about the villages, teaching. (Mark 6:1-6)

The people of Nazareth acknowledged that miracles and healings took place through the ministry of Jesus. Yet they did not consider or respect Him as a prophet. He was merely "Joseph's son." This attitude of disrespect brought very minor results from Jesus, though He was the same man with the same anointing and message as in other cities. How you receive or honor is how you will be rewarded.

Many say they honor God, but show no honor toward their man or woman of God. Can you honor God without honoring the gift He has placed in your midst?

> ***If a man say, I love God, and hateth his brother, he is a liar: for he that loveth not his brother whom he hath seen, how can he love God whom he hath not seen?*** *And this commandment have we from him, That he who loveth God love his brother also. (1 John 4:20-21)*

John uses this verse to offer a principle that can be applied to most any area of our life. He notes that you cannot love God, Whom you cannot see, if you cannot love your brother or sister, whom you can see. The same holds true for honor. If you cannot honor your spiritual father, whom you can see, you cannot truly honor God, Whom you cannot see. Some would argue, but the scriptures are clear.

Biblical Honor

We see examples throughout the Old and New Testaments of how we are to honor God and men and women of God. Through these passages of scripture we can see the Biblical way to honor those in our midst. As we do so, the rewards will come.

God said we are to honor Him by giving the first part of all our increase.

> ***Honour the LORD with thy substance, and with the firstfruits of all thine increase: So shall thy barns be filled with plenty, and thy presses shall burst out with new wine. (Proverbs 3:9-10)***

When honoring a man or woman of God, we are also given a pattern to be followed...

> ***And he said unto him, <u>Behold now, there is in this city a man of God, and he is an honourable man; all that he saith cometh surely to pass</u>: now let us go thither; peradventure he can shew us our way that we should go. <u>Then said Saul to his servant, But, behold, if we go, what shall we bring the man? for the bread is spent in our vessels, and there is not a present to bring to the man of God: what have we? And the servant answered Saul again, and said, Behold, I have here at hand the fourth part of a shekel</u>***

> ***of silver: that will I give to the man of God,***
> ***to tell us our way.*** *(1 Samuel 9:6-8)*

Saul needed help finding a lost animal and became aware of a man of God in a nearby city. Notice his first question, *"...behold, if we go, what shall we bring the man?"* Saul was not offering to pay for the services of the prophet, he was showing honor to the gift in the man. In this example, his honor was demonstrated through his sowing of finances into the life of the prophet.

The New Testament continues this thought, that honor and material blessing go hand in hand. Notice First Timothy 5:17...

> ***Let the elders (ministers) that rule well be***
> ***counted worthy of double honour, especially***
> ***they who labour in the word and doctrine.***

The word *honor*, according to the *Greek Dictionary of the New Testament*, means "value", "money paid", "valuables", "esteem" and "dignity." No, it's not all about money, but it is all about honor.

> *"Honor is not merely financial."*

Honor is not merely financial. What about manners and courtesy? What about not doing all the talking when you are around your spiritual father and not interrupting or trying to talk over him when he is speaking?

> *For God commanded, saying, <u>Honour thy</u>*
> *<u>father and mother</u>: and, He that curseth*
> *father or mother, let him die the death.*
> *(Matthew 15:4)*

The word *father* in this verse means a "spiritual father" according to *Greek Lexical Aids to the New Testament #3962*. Honoring your spiritual father is a commandment.

We need to understand Hebrews 3:3 that says, *"...he who hath builded the house hath more honour than the house."* This word *honor* is the same as mentioned in First Timothy 5:17. Remember, every house is built by a man. (Hebrews 3:4) You and I are houses, spiritually speaking, that have been built by others. Others who have spoken to, cared for, prayed for, and ministered impartations to us. We must

> *"Honor is a matter of sowing and reaping."*

never forget that the person who has "built" us up spiritually and cared for our life has more honor than a building or some other material thing.

Honor is a matter of sowing and reaping. Most believers have some understanding of this system. They make the mistake, however, of believing this principle applies only to finances. Harvests can come in many forms; peace, health, and stability are just a few. Honor can also be sown and reaped. In the same way that a seed of grain can be sown into the earth, honor can be sown. It is not sown into the same ground as a grain of wheat, it is sown into someone's life. The field into which we are to sow is our spiritual father.

Am I not an apostle? am I not free? have I not seen Jesus Christ our Lord? <u>are not ye my work in the Lord? If I be not an apostle unto others, yet doubtless I am to you: for the seal of mine apostleship are ye in the Lord.</u> ...Who goeth a warfare any time at his own charges? who planteth a vineyard, and eateth not of the fruit thereof? or who feedeth a flock, and eateth not of the milk of the flock? <u>...If we have sown unto you spiritual things, is it a great thing if we shall reap your carnal things? If others be partakers of this power over you, are not we rather?</u> Nevertheless we have not used this power; but suffer all things, lest we should hinder the gospel of Christ. <u>Do ye not know that they which minister about holy things live of the things of the temple? and they which wait at the altar are partakers with the altar? Even so hath the Lord ordained that they which preach the gospel should live of the gospel.</u> (1 Corinthians 9:1-2, 7, 11-14)

I am the fruit of my spiritual father's loins. I am not taking God out of the equation, but a man is necessary for spiritual fruit to remain in this earth. If I have reaped from the word as taught by my spiritual father, am I not responsible to sow back into that land? It is ordained that those who preach the Gospel are to make a living of the Gospel. If I have benefited from the word preached by my father, I must demonstrate honor by sowing back into that word. (Galatians 6:6) Do people eat at one restaurant and pay at another? Do they purchase a vehicle and pay for it at the dry cleaners? We pay where we have received the service. I sow honor not by compulsion, but by spiritual law. I honor the labor of my father as an act of my *free will.* I greatly appreciate the sacrifices that he has made to bring me the uncompromised Word of God.

> *"I am the fruit of my spiritual father's loins. I am not taking God out of the equation, but a man is necessary for spiritual fruit to remain in this earth."*

Impartations

8

For I long to see you, <u>that I may impart unto</u>
<u>you some spiritual gift</u>, to the end ye may be
established; That is, that I may be comforted
together with you by the mutual faith both
of you and me. (Romans 1:11-12)

This verse in Romans emphasizes the importance of being present when the one to whom you are submitted is ministering. We can get something through CDs, books, and DVDs, but there is something special and unique about being *present* with your spiritual father.

Impartations come to us through our spiritual fathers and help take us to the next level. These impartations can give us new equipment or enhance the spiritual equipment we already have. Sometimes there will be callings, anointings, and mantles that lie dormant. Spiritual fathers impart power that causes movement and increase, much like a chemical catalyst that causes change when added. After an impartation we are suddenly aware of, have a new sensitivity toward, and enjoy a new accuracy towards the things of the spirit.

I remember being with Dr. Dufresne, my spiritual father, in Abakan, Russia. It was *life* changing. I received so much and I have never been the same. I received an impartation. My hunger for the Word of God became even

> "Who are these men?"

stronger. Since that trip my preaching and ministering has taken on a different anointing. Below is part of a prophetic word that came forth from Dr. Dufresne as we sat in a side room and shook under the power of God after an evening service in Abakan, Russia...

"Who are these men? They can tell me about my past and they can tell me about my future? Who are these men that are moving across this land with the power of God...doing the acts of God? ...These are the men that I will send all over the world with special anointings. Special anointings, special works of God; special acts of God will flow through their ministries. ...Who are these men? ...These are the men that will walk in the power of the acts of God and the healings of God. And they will move across this land...this generation. There will be a generation raised up for miracles, signs, and wonders. ...Who are these men? When they go into cities and churches raise up right away. Right away. I'll tell you who these men

are. These are the men of these days that are anointed by the power of God-to do the acts of-who yield themselves to the acts of God."

In Romans 1:11, Paul talks about imparting *spiritual gifts.* The word for *gift* in the Greek means "a spiritual endowment", "a miraculous faculty", "a deliverance or rescue." Paul was imparting out of his endowment from God to others. It was from a *supernatural* source. It was a miraculous faculty. It provided deliverance and a rescue for the people to whom he imparted. John Wesley's personal notes on Romans 1:11 say, *"Impartations can come*

> *"...These are the men that I will send all over the world with special anointings. "*

through prayer, preaching, laying on of hands, and private conversations. " I can personally testify to this operation coming to me from my spiritual father over and over again.

I remember traveling to Temecula, California to attend Dr. Dufresne's Fresh Oil Conference in 1995. I was in the meeting and the Lord said, *"Sow $1000.00 into this ministry."* I didn't have $50.00 at the time! I raised my hand and on an offering envelope wrote, *"I pledge $1000.00 when it comes in. "*

> *"...special acts of God will flow through their ministries."*

Within a year I received the money to meet my pledge and the day after was having lunch with Dr.

Dufresne. I handed him my check and fire shot out of his eyes. He said, *"I'm speaking to you as a prophet, you'll come out of debt and the pain in your side will leave."* (I was $20,000.00 in debt due to medical bills. I had a pain in my side for fourteen years and although the doctors performed many tests on numerous hospital visits, they were to no avail. *But an impartation...*) Within three months all the medical debt was paid. Within the year I got up one morning and the pain was gone. I had received a rescue and a deliverance through my man of God. He had equipment in him that helped me. I received from the endowment in him. I received an *impartation.* Remember, Romans 1:11-12 says it takes mutual faith. You have to believe what is ministered *will come to pass.* You must believe you receive *when* you are prayed for or ministered to.

> *"I had received a rescue and a deliverance through my man of God. ...I received an impartation."*

Many times I have been delivered, rescued, and ministered to by my spiritual father. All of these times have been special and precious to me. These impartations have strengthened me, corrected my thinking, and changed the course of my ministry. The impartations received from Dr. Dufresne have caused me to become more focused, more accurate, and definitely more anointed as I have yielded and obeyed. I am so thankful for all the counsel, care, and time spent with my spiritual father.

I recall another time when I had gone to my doctor for a physical. The doctor was concerned about some test results and said there was something wrong with my blood. He asked if I would come back and give more blood for additional testing. I agreed, but explained that it would be a week before I could return. I had planned to call Dr. Dufresne and ask for his agreement in prayer, but decided to speak to him in person. I was going to Birmingham, Alabama in a few days to hear him speak and thought I would talk with him about it then. You see, I had been a drug dealer and shot dope for several years in the late sixties and early seventies. In 1972 I had Hepatitis C and was healed though I had no treatment whatsoever. You can understand why this could have been a serious situation in the natural realm. Of course, we are called to walk by faith and look to the Word of God for our answers. (Hebrews 12:2)

> *"These impartations have strengthened me, corrected my thinking, and changed the course of my ministry."*

I arrived in Birmingham the first night of the meeting and had not yet spoken to Dr. Dufresne about the report I had been given. Dr. Dufresne was preaching and suddenly stopped. He said, *"Pastor Jacobs, where are you?"* I raise my hand because I was about ten rows from the front. He said, *"Step out in the aisle. The Lord shows me you have something wrong with your body. Is that right?"* I said, *"Yes sir."* He said, *"There is*

an angel standing behind you now and he is going to fix that."
I felt the power of God come on me and I fell on the floor. When
I went home to my doctor, he took more blood. He later called
and said that my blood looked perfect. I was *with* my spiritual
father and he helped *perfect* something.

> **Night and day praying exceedingly that we**
> **might see your face, _and might perfect that_**
> **_which is lacking in your faith?_**
> **_(1 Thessalonians 3:10)_**

I sometimes feel like the writer of Hebrews when he said,
And what shall I more say? for the time would fail me to tell
of all that has happened in my life for good since I found my
spiritual father.

Our Own Souls

Some say that I sometimes act and sound like my spiritual
father. I am thankful and thrilled for such compliments. The Word
of God indicates that this takes place because it is not only the
spoken word that is imparted. There is also an imparting of the
speaker's soul.

> **So being affectionately desirous of you, we**
> **were willing to have _imparted unto you, not_**
> **_the gospel of God only, but also our own_**

***souls, because ye were dear unto us.
(1 Thessalonians 2:8)***

I am thankful for all I have received. I thank you Dr. Dufresne for all you have done for me. Through your preaching, your prayers, your private counsel, and the laying on of your hands. Thank you Dr. Dufresne for all you have put in me. I will forever be grateful. God hooked us up supernaturally. It has been and is a divine connection that continues to grow richer and fuller day by day.

About the Author

Dr. Michael P. Jacobs is founding pastor of Church on the Rock in New Albany, Indiana and has been in ministry since 1973. Along with authoring several books, including *Angels on Earth, They are Waiting on You*, Dr. Jacobs serves as a board member of Dr. Ed Dufresne's "Fresh Oil Fellowship." A pastor to several pastors and missionaries, Dr. Jacobs has ministered on more than 75 mission trips and travels extensively throughout the United States ministering the Word of God. Physical healings, deliverance, and a tangible anointing are evident in his meetings. His wife, Diana, his daughter and son-in-law, Jessica and Jacob, and his son and daughter-in-law, Jordan and Lauren, are also involved with him in the ministry.

If you would like to contact the author, please write:
Church on the Rock
Attn: Dr. Michael P. Jacobs
4224 Mel Smith Road
New Albany, Indiana 47150
or call: (812) 948-5906, or e-mail: cotr@insightbb.com

Please include your testimony or help received from this book when you write.

Additional Materials

Michael Jacobs Ministries *(Materials available in Spanish*)*

Book:
Angels on Earth: They are Waiting on You*
Spiritual Father or Spiritual Failure*

DVD Materials:
Angels on Earth   Angels on Earth Series
Hope   Ministering Spirits and Healing
Personal Angels   Somebody is Anointed to Help You
What Angels Do

Compact Disc Materials:
2010 Prayer Conference   A Belief System in Healing
A Fresh Anointing   Activate Your Angels
Adventures in Faith   Angels on Earth
Applying the Blood of Jesus   Authority of the Believer
Being Filled with the Spirit   Can a Christian Have a Demon?
Covenant Relationships   Cultivating Spiritual Endowments
Demonology   Discerning of Spirits
Drugs and Alcoholism   Faith has a Voice
Fellowshiping with the Father   Get Connected
Gold, Guys/Girls, Glory   Guidelines for Ministers
Having and Enjoying Long Life   Healing is God's Will for You
House of Faith   How Far Does the Blood Go?
Impartations   Job

Joy-Don't Drop Your Bucket   Laying on of Hands
Learn to Sense What is Vital   Living Fearlessly
Living in the Supernatural   Man's Authority Restored
Ministering Spirits and Money   Ministering Spirits are with Us
Nashville Healing Conference   Nature of Demons
Origin of the Devil and Demons   Our Authority with Angels
Paul's Thorn   Personal Angels
Protecting Divine Supplies   Recognizing Demonic Influence
Redemption   Somebody is Anointed to Help You
Spiritual Father or Spiritual Failure   Spirit of Jezebel
Stay with It   Taking Care of Your Man of God
The Word of Knowledge   Things that Angels Do
Working of Miracles   Your Future is in Your Mouth

Additional Materials

Book:

How to Receive Your Divine Supply by B. Shaun Garing
Sheep, Bellsheep, and Sheep Dogs by B. Shaun Garing
Understanding the Gift in Your Pastor by B. Shaun Garing